C000006263

Exmoor
pub walks

Robert Hesketh

Bossiney Books • Launceston

Some other Bossiney walks books

North Dartmoor pub walks
South Dartmoor pub walks

Shortish walks on Exmoor
Shortish walks on Dartmoor
Shortish walks in east Devon
Shortish walks in north Devon
Shortish walks – The Levels and south Somerset

First published 2008 by
Bossiney Books Ltd, Langore, Launceston, Cornwall PL15 8LD
www.bossineybooks.com
© 2008 Robert Hesketh   All rights reserved
ISBN 978-1-899383-97-9

Acknowledgements
The maps are by Graham Hallowell
Cover based on a design by Heards Design Partnership
Photographs by the author except pages 5, 9, 11, 13, 15, 19, 25, 27 and 31,
which are from the publishers' own collection

Printed in Great Britain by R Booth Ltd, Mabe, Cornwall

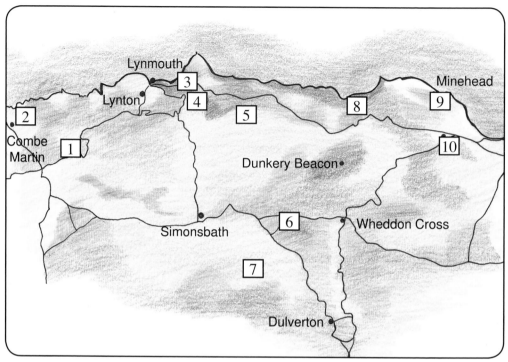

The approximate locations of the starting point for the walks in this book

Introduction

Exmoor is a walker's paradise, criss-crossed with well signed walks and a great variety of scenery in a relatively small area. High moorland and sea cliffs, rolling hills cut by fast flowing rivers and steep, wooded valleys – the moor is endlessly enjoyable. It also has its own breed of wild pony and is the last stronghold of England's largest mammal, the red deer.

A great complement to a good walk is a good pub. Exmoor has some of the best. Each of these walks includes at least one pub, with notes on its name, history and special features. In several cases these include deer-hunting. Exmoor Forest was a royal hunting preserve, and riding and the hunting tradition remain central to local life.

At between 9km and 15km (5 1/2 and 9 1/4 miles), all the routes can be walked in a day. Some could be completed in a morning or afternoon, though it is best to start with the shorter walks if you are out of practice to build your stamina. The time you need depends on how fast you walk and how interested you are in what you see – and each

walk has several extras, from historic churches to prehistoric monuments.

Safety (please take seriously)

Walking Exmoor is safe and trouble-free – but be prepared, especially for sudden changes in the weather. Despite a generally mild climate, high winds and fogs are not unknown – not to mention rain! Good walking boots and suitable clothing, including waterproofs, are a must – so are drinking water, a map (Ordnance Survey OL9), compass and a comfortable rucksack. Many, including me, add a walking stick, mobile phone and food to the list.

Ticks are a potential nuisance, especially in hot, humid weather. Wearing long trousers and socks offers some protection against these tiny parasites, which can carry a viral infection, Lyme disease.

Access

Unenclosed moorland areas are generally open. Please keep to the paths over enclosed farmland, use (and close) gates as appropriate and keep dogs under control.

I am sure you will enjoy these walks as I have.

Robert Hesketh

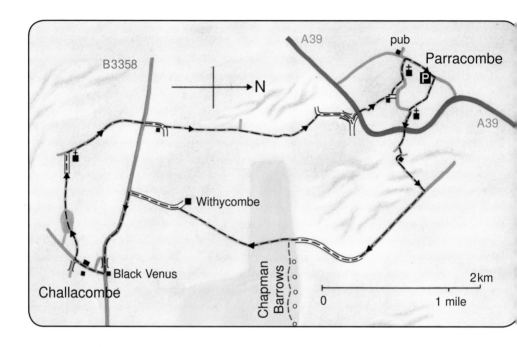

Walk 1 Parracombe and Challacombe

Distance: 15 km (9¹/₄ miles) Time: 4¹/₂ hours
Character: Mostly field paths and some open moor, but also 1 km along
a B-road. Some long steady climbs but no really demanding slopes. The
walk connects two attractive Exmoor villages, each with a historic
church and inn. There are magnificent views, as well as a group of
prehistoric burial mounds and a view of a Norman motte and bailey
castle (see photo opposite). A compass may be useful.

Start from Parracombe's car park, 100 m uphill from Bodley Cross
and just downhill from Heddon Hall. Walk uphill for 150 m and take
the footpath on the right. This emerges by a bridge spanning the old
Lynton & Barnstaple Railway.

Turn left, PUBLIC BRIDLEWAY A39. Follow the bridleway uphill, pass-
ing St Petrock's church (unspoilt Georgian interior). Cross the A39
and take the BRIDLEWAY PARRACOMBE COMMON to a junction 250 m
ahead, and take the left fork (blue waymark).

Turn right at a T-junction of tracks, PARRACOMBE COMMON. Follow
the track past a house and up to another T-junction. Turn right
and follow the straight tarmac drive, later a track, for 2 km over
Parracombe Common to a gate.

Divert left to see Chapman Barrows, one of Exmoor's most impressive groups of Bronze Age burial mounds. Keep the wall on your left and climb the ladder stile at the top corner. The first of the barrows is on the other side. To see more barrows, you could continue in the same direction to the triangulation point on the summit, which would add 1.6 km (a mile) to the length of the walk.

Retrace your steps to the gate and turn left, WITHECOMBE GATE. Walk south over rough grass (the path may well be indistinct) to a gate in the wall ahead. Follow the BRIDLEWAY downhill through several more gates. Pass Withycombe Farm and continue down a concrete track to B3358. Turn left along it for 1.1 km to the Black Venus.

Take the lane opposite the inn and cross the ford 50 m ahead by the footbridge. Walk on past the chapel. At Rooksfoot, a characteristic Exmoor packhorse bridge, turn right, FOOTPATH CHALLACOMBE. Continue via gates and a stile. Bear right (CHALLACOMBE CHURCH) and up through a wood. Cross the fields ahead to the whitewashed church.

Turn right and follow the lane to Yelland Cross. Walk ahead, PUBLIC BRIDLEWAY TWINEWORTHY. Just past the entrance to 'West Whitefield', bear left onto the bridleway as signed, and turn right up the field. Follow the blue waymarks of the bridleway north through

fields, over the rougher grass of Challacombe Common, then down through a sloping field of furze to a metal gate. Now keep the hedge on your left. Reaching a track, turn right BRIDLEWAY.

Follow the track down and over a bridge, then uphill, first curving right then turning sharp left. Cross the A39, FOOTPATH PARRACOMBE. Follow waymarks across the fields to an enclosed lane. Only 40 m ahead, turn left through a gate. Turn right and follow the yellow waymarks along the field edge and into an enclosed lane, for Parracombe.

Go through the yard of Sunnyside Farm, then bear left (PUBLIC FOOTPATH PARRACOMBE) across fields and a stream to Christ Church. The churchyard offers a fine view of Holwell, one of hundreds of Norman motte-and-bailey castles built across England after 1066. Follow the lane downhill to a T-junction. Turn right uphill, past Bodley Cross, to the car park.

The Black Venus 01598 763251

An ancient drovers' inn, the Black Venus may derive its unique name from a breed of sheep, difficult to shear and giving worthless wool. It was formerly the Ring of Bells, as historic photos in the bar show. Note the exposed ceiling beams and the hand-carved fireplace, inscribed 'Welcome all to hearth and hall.'

Walk 2   Combe Martin and the Pack o' Cards

Distance: 8.9km (5¹/₂ miles)   Time: 3 hours
Character: The climb to Great Hangman – at 318m the highest point
on the South West Coast Path – is rewarded with spectacular views.
The return includes old silver mines, a medieval church with a superb
carved screen, and a unique inn.

The Pack o' Cards

The Pack o' Cards was built in 1690 by George Ley, the squire of
Combe Martin. After winning handsomely at cards, he promised 'an
everlasting monument to Lady Luck'. The Pack is inspired by a deck
of 52 playing cards. It is 52ft square, has four storeys to represent
the four suits, 52 windows and 52 steps in the staircase. There are 13
doors on each floor, and 13 fireplaces.

   The four chimneys on the top floor represent the four kings, and
the four chimneys below the four queens. The squire's study has 13
panes of glass, whilst the joker window is incomplete.

   For over a century the Pack was the Leys' family home. It became
an inn during the early nineteenth century: the list of landlords goes
back to 1822. Known as the King's Arms, it did not become the Pack o'
Cards officially until 1933. This fascinating folly was derelict in 1985.
Happily it was restored from 1991, as the inn's museum explains.

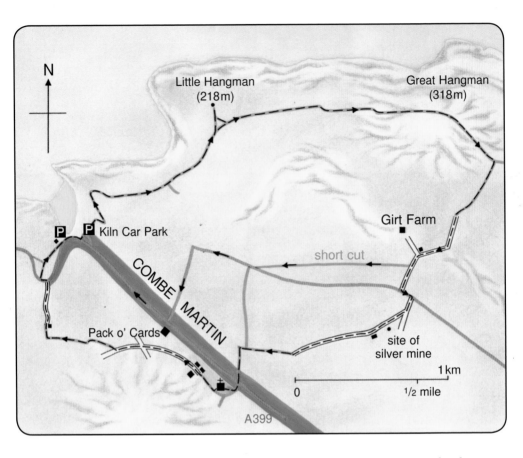

From the Kiln car park at the seaward end of Combe Martin, take the signed coast path towards the east.

Winding around gardens and up onto the cliffs, the path is clear and stepped where really steep. Little Hangman (218m) is reached by a slight diversion from the main path, but gives wonderful views. The path to the cairn on the top of Great Hangman is a gentler ascent.

From there, follow the coast path downhill to a fingerpost set in the corner of a stone wall. Turn right, COUNTY ROAD. Keep the wall on your left. Continue over a stile and into a farm track.

Bear left at a house onto FOOTPATH COMBE MARTIN. Walk up the concrete track to the next fingerpost. (You could take a short cut by turning right, COMBE MARTIN VIA KNAP DOWN LANE, reducing the walk by 1.4km.)

For the full route, continue ahead, SILVER MINES. Turn left at the tarred lane and after 50m turn right down a broad track, PUBLIC

FOOTPATH. When the track divides, bear right. On your left are the ivy-covered remains of the old silver mines (private property). The path descends steeply past Silver Mines Farm, after which it deteriorates. Continue downhill to the town.

Cross HIGH STREET into CHURCH STREET. Turn right up BOWLING GREEN LANE to visit the church. Exit by the lych gate and turn right, PUBLIC FOOTPATH PARK HILLS. This climbs steadily, giving good views of the Hangmen, of Combe Martin's main street, said to be the longest in England, and of the Pack o' Cards.

Fork right from the stony track when a clear level beaten path appears. Do not cross the stile on the right but continue ahead, keeping the hedge on your right. Then turn right through a wicket gate with a footpath sign. Follow the enclosed path downhill to a stile, then continue along the driveway to the main road.

Cross the road and turn left along the grass verge for 30 m, then turn right, PUBLIC FOOTPATH, Keep going downhill, and follow the road out to the main road, then turn left back down to the Kiln car park.

Whilst there are other pubs near the harbour, you will probably want to drive 1 km up the High Street to the Pack o' Cards.

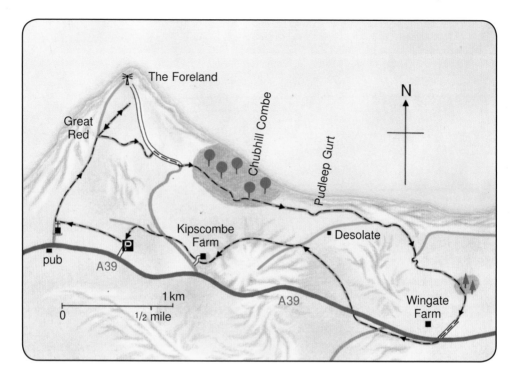

Walk 3   Countisbury

Distance: 11.7km (7¹/₄ miles) including the summit of Foreland
Time: 3³/₄ hours. Can be shortened to 8km (5 miles) or else combined
with Walk 4 to make an all-day walk.

Character: Towering more than 210m above the sea, with dramatic
scree slopes, Foreland Point offers magnificent views and is one of
Exmoor's most impressive sights. The walk also includes a fine section
of the coast path, magnificent rhododendrons in May (in many other
places they have been eradicated as an invasive and destructive weed)
and a pleasant inland return. One steep ascent.

Start from the National Trust's Barna Barrow car park (SS753496).
With your back to the road, turn left and follow the path with the
stone wall on your left. After visiting the church, either take the south
gate to visit the Exmoor Sandpiper or leave by the north gate and take
the COASTPATH north along the contour of the cliffs. Continue ahead
at the next path junction, PORLOCK.

A deep gash in the cliffs is called Great Red. Turn right, COASTPATH
LIGHTHOUSE, or follow the rough path to the crest of the cliffs for the
best views, then retrace your steps to continue along the coast path.

10

Follow the path downhill to a tarred lane. Unless you wish to divert left along the lane to the lighthouse, turn right and follow the lane uphill. At the top of the slope, walk ahead COASTPATH. The path continues over a stile and on to Glenthorne Cliffs and Chubhill Wood, where gnarled oaks cling bravely to the scree slopes.

Beyond Chubhill Wood, choose either the short cut COUNTISBURY, reducing the walk by 2.5km (1 1/2 miles) and rejoin the directions where asterisked, or continue along the coastpath for the full route.

Turn right off the coastpath at the next fingerpost, by a brook WHITE GATE COUNTY GATE. Follow the yellow waymarks up a steep slope. Continue across a field and through a conifer plantation. Bear right at the next fingerpost, WINGATE FARM. The path emerges onto the main road. Cross, and turn right COUNTISBURY along the wide verge. Pass the BRENDON turn, then at the fingerpost FOOTPATH BARNA BARROW, cross the road and a stile.

Walk ahead, following yellow waymarks and keeping the wall on your right, to join the short cut * at a footpath junction. Walk on through fields (i.e. turn right if you used the short cut) and around the back of Kipscombe Farm (to the left of the trees). Take the footpath ahead, COUNTISBURY, keeping the field edge on your right.

11

Cross a tarmac lane and walk ahead for 50 m. Fork left where the track divides. Fork left again at the next path division and continue over open moorland to the car park.

To visit the Exmoor Sandpiper, either retrace your steps to Countisbury or collect your car and drive down to the inn's car park.

The Exmoor Sandpiper 01598 741263 www.exmoor-sandpiper.co.uk

Standing on the A39 Exmoor coast road, an old coaching route, the Exmoor Sandpiper has been dated to approximately 1300 by the cavernous fireplace, where a hearty fire burns all year. It has a bread oven and cooking jacks.

Like many ancient buildings, the inn has been much altered over time, with 16th century additions at the east end and 18th century additions at the west end. Between 1800 and 1896 it was known as the Blue Ball Inn. After a year as the Blue Boar, it became the Exmoor Sandpiper.

The Common sandpiper, nearly always seen along the water margins and known for its clear piping tone, is mainly a spring and autumn visitor but apparently occasionally over-winters in the South-West.

Walk 4   Watersmeet and the Rockford Inn

Distance: 8.1km (5 miles) Time: 2³/₄ hours
Character: Two steep ascents and one steep descent are amply
rewarded by spectacular views of two deep river gorges and the rocky
coast. This is one of the West Country's most beautiful riverside walks.
It could be linked with Walk 3.

The Rockford Inn (01598 741214, closed Mondays) is thought to be 17th century, but has been altered over the years. It has a fine collection of local period photographs; one shows the landlord and landlady of 1906. There are also murals by local artist Mick Cawston depicting Exmoor wildlife. With two wood-burning stoves it is very cosy inside, and there is also a small beer garden overlooking the river. Beer brewed on the premises is a special feature.

Also on the route are the Exmoor Sandpiper (see opposite page) and a National Trust tearooms. You will not want to be rushed on this walk, so you could make it a long day out with several refreshment stops. In that case you might want to start from the free car park at Countisbury, though be warned: that makes the final part of the walk a long steep ascent.

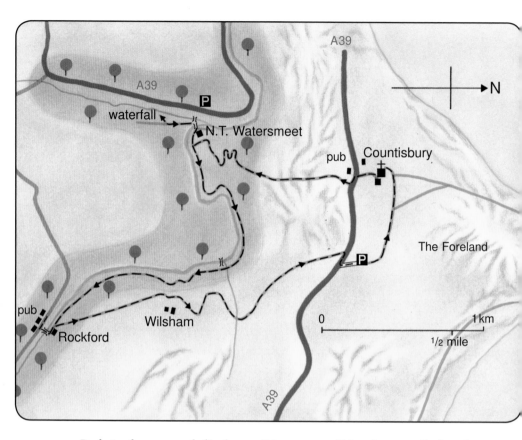

Park in the pay-and-display at Watersmeet. Take the gravelled path downhill. Cross a footbridge and divert right up steps, WATERFALL VIEWPOINT. After seeing the waterfall, retrace your steps to the footbridge. Do not return across it, but turn right and cross a second bridge to the National Trust's shop/tearoom/information centre – formerly a shooting and fishing lodge.

The scene is most dramatic after heavy rain, with the river in spate. However, no one would wish for a repeat of the 1952 flood. Over 225mm (9 inches) had fallen on Exmoor in two days. Spates rushed down both the East and West Lyn. Powered by more water than flows down the Thames in three months, the flood swept away houses and cars and killed 34 people.

Leaving the tearoom, turn left upriver, soon signed FISHERMAN'S PATH ROCKFORD & BRENDON. Continue for some 2.25km along the riverbank. Pass Rockford Lodge, then cross the footbridge about 100m further on. Turn right to visit the Rockford Inn.

14

Now retrace your steps to Rockford Lodge, and turn right, COUNTISBURY VIA WILSHAM. Walk up through the trees and continue ahead on FOOTPATH WILSHAM WALKERS ONLY. At the T-junction ahead, keep left and follow the series of yellow waymarks north, one marked COUNTISBURY. After winding round Wilsham, the path descends to a brook, then climbs steeply to the A39.

Turn right up the road for 60 m, then left into and through the National Trust car park. Keep the wall on your left and follow the path round to Countisbury church. Walk through the churchyard and down towards the Exmoor Sandpiper. Turn left up the main road for 60 m.

Turn right, WATERSMEET VIA TRILLY RIDGE. Follow the walled path to a field. Continue ahead, WATERSMEET. Keep the wall 50 m to your left to find a path downhill through the furze, and through a gate to a footpath junction. Continue ahead, WATERSMEET. The path soon descends very steeply through dense woodland. At a T-junction, turn sharp right and continue downhill to Watersmeet. Retrace your steps across the footbridges to the car park.

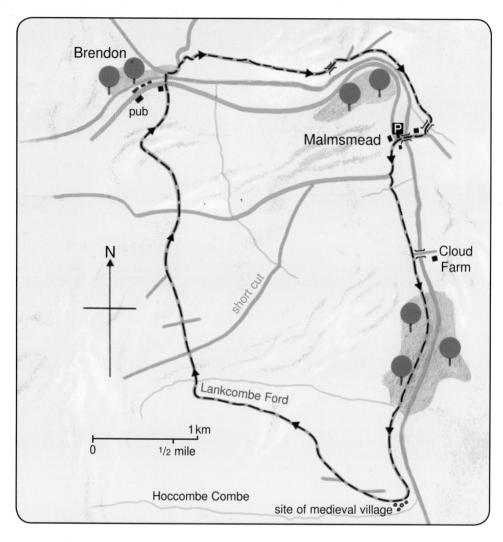

Walk 5 Malmsmead and Badgeworthy

Distance: 14km (8½ miles) Time: 4½ hours
Character: This classic walk has all the vital Exmoor ingredients:
windswept moorland, deep wooded valleys cut by sparkling rivers and
a patchwork of green fields with the restless sea beyond. The route
includes a deserted medieval village, used as the stronghold of the
Doones, the dastardly robber band, by R D Blackmore in his celebrated
Exmoor novel Lorna Doone. *A relatively easy walk for the distance,*
the route has one steep ascent and two steep descents. Map and
compass essential.

From Lorna Doone Farm at Malmsmead – the probable original for Jan Ridd's home in the novel – take LANE LEADING TO PUBLIC FOOTPATH DOONE VALLEY (or pay 50p and use the riverbank path). After 250m bear left, BRIDLEWAY DOONE VALLEY.

At Cloud Farm (teas and lunches) continue ahead BRIDLEWAY DOONE VALLEY, following the river for 2.5km.

Just beyond the next sign, BRENDON COMMON LARKBARROW, the path curves right. On the left is an abandoned medieval village. Its bracken-covered ruins are typical of local longhouses, with one room for the farmer's family and one for the animals. It has decayed greatly since Blackmore wrote *Lorna Doone* in 1869 – you need imagination to see the Doones in all their wicked splendour.

Return to the track, which rises steadily, curving gently away from Hoccombe Combe. When the track divides, keep right on the better used fork. Several roughly parallel tracks converge to ford the stream at Lankcombe Combe. At the crossways ahead, you could take a short cut by turning right, MALMSMEAD, on a bridleway which cuts northeast across Malmsmead Hill, where you turn right onto Post Lane and follow it to the start. (We have not checked this route recently.)

For the full route continue ahead, BRIDLEWAY BRENDON and enjoy the view. At the next signpost continue ahead, BRIDLEWAY BRENDON, and again for BRENDON when you reach Cross Gate on a tarred lane.

Stag Hunters Hotel

01598 741222

www.staghunters.com

The Stag Hunters is thought to have been an inn since the 18th century.

Originally the Abbey Inn, so-called from the 15th century chapel at the east end, the Stag Hunters has local photographs and trophies of the chase. The character portrait shows farm labourer Johnny Coward, who entertained visitors and won pints with entirely fictitious accounts of his life as a jockey, before being taken home by his still sober pony.

Descend to the village. To visit the Stag Hunters, turn left at Leeford Green, SIMONSBATH BARNSTAPLE. Retrace your steps to Leeford Green. Turn left LYNMOUTH, cross the bridge and turn right, PORLOCK.

Follow the lane to a ladder stile, FOOTPATH COUNTY GATE MALMSMEAD. The path winds uphill, then follows the side of the valley giving dramatic views.

Cross a footbridge and turn left, following the curving path uphill. At the top of the rise the path divides. Keep right, on the lower path, go through a gate and take the lower path, MALMSMEAD OARE.

Descend to the river and follow the bankside path round to the second footbridge, with a yellow waymark. Cross and walk up to the tarred lane. Turn right and follow the lane back to Lorna Doone Farm.

Walk 6 Exford and the Exe Valley

Distance: 9.2km (5³/4 miles) Time: 3 hours
Character: A first class Exmoor route which offers great views and
combines moorland rambling with a beautiful riverside path. Watch
out for deer. The walk follows bridleways and footpaths, with one steep
ascent and one steep descent – with loose stones, so take care.

The Exmoor White Horse (01643) 831229

Exford's White Horse is said to date from the 16th century. Country
sports are well represented, with a magnificent stag's head in the hall
and a collection of photos in the large bar, plus trophies of the chase.
The dining room has many landscape colour photographs, mainly
local scenes, by the landlord.

Start from Exford's car park (SS853384). Follow the sign PUBLIC
FOOTPATH LYNCOMBE/ROOM HILL and continue for 400m along the
east bank of the river. Cross the bridge to Court Farm. Turn left,
BRIDLEWAY TO WITHYPOOL VIA ROOM HILL. Follow the track around
the farm. When the lane bends sharp right, bear left through a gate,
BRIDLEWAY ROOM HILL.

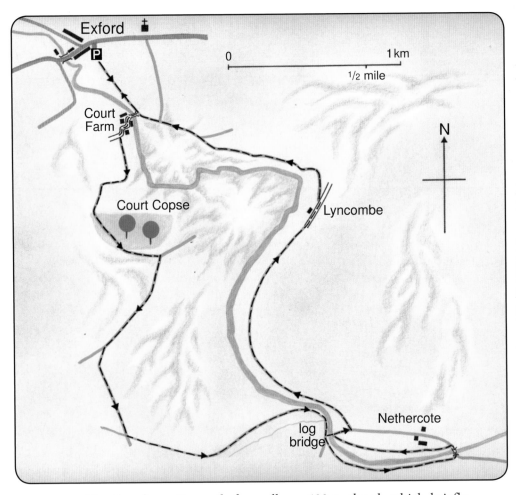

Use the alternative path for walkers, 400 m ahead, which briefly avoids a muddy stretch of the bridleway then rejoins the main path at a gate. Continue steeply uphill. Extensive views open up as the path leaves Court Copse.

At the signed bridleway junction, turn right and continue uphill through a characteristic Exmoor beech hedgebank. Continue on level ground. Keep left when the track forks, around the head of a deep wooded valley. Keep left again after 450 m, WINSFORD.

Continue ahead, ignoring side turnings, to a beech hedge and gate. Don't go through the gate but turn left, downhill, with the hedge on your right, to meet a well defined bridleway, which keeps to the left of a steep gully. Follow it down to the river, turn right and continue for 50 m.

If you wish to cut the route short by 1.6km (1 mile), cross the river by the log and wire bridge. The main route rejoins you immediately on the other side at point *.

Otherwise, turn right through a gate then keep the fence on your left, following the permitted footpath for 800m along the southern bank of the river, to a concrete bridge.

Cross over, and turn left through the meadows, PERMITTED FOOTPATH EXFORD. (After very wet weather, take the bridleway past East and West Nethercote. This is the route shown on OS maps.) Follow the riverside path to a gate near the log and wire bridge *.

Turn right uphill. After 50m turn sharp left onto a broad path. Continue on this path to Lyncombe.

Just beyond Lyncombe, turn left over a stile, FOOTPATH ONLY. This leads to a ford. Don't cross the river, but turn right along the east bank path. Cross three stiles in quick succession and follow the path as it diverges from the river and climbs.

Don't take the footpath to the church. Reaching the bridge to Court Farm, retrace your steps to the car park.

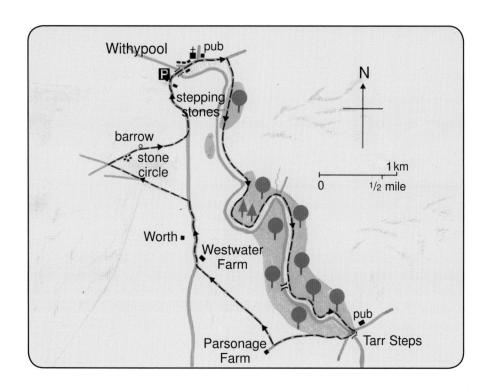

Walk 7   Withypool and Tarr Steps

Distance: 13.4km (8¹/₄ miles)   Time: 4¹/₄ hours
Character: This superb Exmoor walk combines a beautiful riverbank path with open moorland, field paths and quiet lanes. As well as Tarr Steps, one of the moor's most fascinating historic structures, there is a prehistoric stone circle and also a barrow on Withypool Hill. At 398m, the hill offers wonderful panoramic views. Three steep ascents. Some parts can be very muddy after rain. Do not attempt this walk if the river is in spate. Take a compass.

Turn left out of the free car park in Withypool (SS 845354). Cross the bridge, built in traditional fashion in 1866. Continue past the post office stores and the church with its curiously squat tower. Walk on past the Royal Oak and follow the lane uphill. Cross a stile on the right, TARR STEPS. Simply follow the path parallel to the River Barle for the next 5.7km, ignoring side turnings, to Tarr Steps.

Tarr Steps is immediately impressive. This 36m long clapper bridge is built of 17 flat slabs of stone, each weighing two tonnes and over two metres long. Most authorities now agree that the present structure

22

is medieval. To the left of Tarr Steps is Tarr Farm, now an inn and restaurant offering refreshments all year.

Cross Tarr Steps and fork right almost immediately, PUBLIC BRIDLEWAY WITHYPOOL HILL. Follow the blue waymarks and stony track steeply uphill, swinging right then turning left before a field gate. Continue uphill then gently down towards Parsonage Farm (refreshments).

Turn right, WITHYPOOL HILL, at the gate leading to Parsonage Farm. Follow the track through a series of fields and gates with blue waymarks. Great views of the Barle Valley and surrounding moorland open up. Walk ahead, WITHYPOOL, at the next signpost.

Arriving at a lane, turn right, WITHYPOOL HILL. Follow the lane past Westwater Farm and uphill to a cattle grid. Turn left, BRIDLEWAY WITHYPOOL HILL. Follow the track, keeping the hedge on your left until it ends. Keep right when the bridleway forks. After 550 m a fainter track crosses the bridleway at an angle.

Turn sharp right and follow it uphill. Aim for the mound on the summit and follow the rough path past a stone circle. If you have a GPS, the circle is at SS 83835 34320. It can easily be missed as the stones are very low and several are missing or buried. Enjoy the views from the barrow on the summit, then follow the rough path eastward. Turn left onto a lane and follow it downhill to the start.

The Royal Oak 01643 831506/7

This fine sporting inn has a traditional character. Trophies of the chase, sporting prints, hunting and wildlife photographs decorate both bars, which have open fires and comfortable seats and tables. There is also a separate dining/function room. The building is thought to be over 300 years old and retains its old fireplaces and exposed ceiling beams. A period photograph in the bar shows the exterior little altered.

Perhaps drawn by its quiet and isolated position, several distinguished and unexpected people have been associated with the Royal Oak. R D Blackmore wrote part of *Lorna Doone* in the bar; the artist Alfred Munnings had a studio in the loft, and General Eisenhower planned parts of the D-Day landings here.

From 1927-35, Gwladys and Maxwell Knight owned the inn. Knight was a bit different from the average innkeeper. Later known to millions as a TV and radio naturalist, he also had a secret career with MI5, which he joined in 1925. Knight became a spy-master at the heart of events and played a key counter-espionage role before and during the Second World War, infiltrating both the Communist Party and Oswald Mosley's British Union of Fascists.

One of Knight's agents was Ian Fleming, who modelled the character M in his James Bond stories on his boss, whose real life story far outshines Fleming's fiction. Ask at the bar to see Knight's portrait.

Walk 8   Bossington and Porlock

Distance: 10km (6¹/₄ miles) Time: 3 hours
Character: Although mainly level, this walk offers great views of
Porlock Bay and the surrounding hills. Since floods broke through the
bay's pebble ridge in 1996, it is no longer possible to walk its entire
length but much of it can be explored from the marsh path described
here. Note that this path should be avoided during high tides and after
heavy rain. There are three attractive villages on the way.

The Ship Inn, Porlock 01643 862507 www.shipinnporlock.co.uk
The sea once came right up to the school opposite. Said to date from
1290, this is one of England's oldest inns, with a thatched roof, exposed
beams, gothic window, huge open fireplaces and a 'lateral' chimneystack
(placed in the side wall rather than end wall). 'Southey's Corner' is
located in this chimneystack, honouring Poet Laureate Robert Southey
who wrote a sonnet celebrating Porlock at the Ship in 1798.

Licencees of the Ship have been traced back to 1744, when most
travellers arrived on foot or horseback, or by boat, and wheeled trans-
port was virtually unknown on Exmoor. With the coming of turnpike
roads and stagecoaches, stabling was developed at the Ship, which
provided extra horses to drag coaches up notorious Porlock Hill.

Modern travellers enjoy log fires in winter and a delightful beer
garden/children's play area in summer.

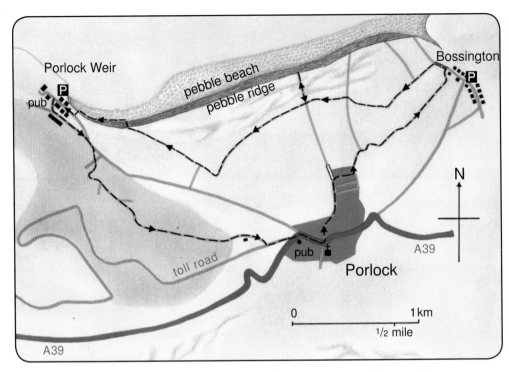

Park in the National Trust car park at Bossington. Turn right out of the car park, COAST PATH PORLOCK WEIR. Keep right at Myrtle Cottage. Follow the lane to a path junction and continue ahead COAST PATH PORLOCK WEIR. Turn left 100 m ahead, COAST PATH PORLOCK WEIR VIA MARSH. Follow the signed coast path with its yellow way-marks and/or acorn signs.

A display board tells the story of the pebble ridge. Formed 8000 years ago by rising sea levels, it was breached in 1996 and subsequent storms have moved the beach 20-30 m inland, cutting a canyon through the marsh clay and turning freshwater marsh into tidal marsh, which is often visited by shelducks, oystercatchers, gulls and curlews.

Unless the tide is high, divert right at the display board to view the pebble ridge from its crest, then retrace your steps to the display board and turn right for PORLOCK WEIR. On the way are a number of skeletons of trees killed by the invading salt.

Follow COAST PATH PORLOCK WEIR VIA MARSH at the next junction (or divert inland WEST PORLOCK if the marsh is flooded). The path briefly crosses onto the beach. Then join the road and continue to Porlock Weir with its pretty harbour.

Facing the Ship Inn, take the lane uphill past the telephone booth. Continue ahead at the junction and past cottages to a T-junction.

Turn right, and after just 75m right again onto an unsigned but obvious footpath. Cross a lane and follow the well-beaten path and various PORLOCK signs through the woods to join another lane, which leads down to the Ship.

Continue past the Ship and follow Porlock's main street, past the church, noted for its shingled spire and handsome monuments. Take the next turning left, SPARKHAYES LANE. Continue ahead past side-streets and a no-through-road sign. When you reach a sign FOOTPATH BEACH NO CARS, turn right up steps and into a street. At the far end turn left, BOSSINGTON.

Keep right at the path junction, BOSSINGTON. Turn right at the next path junction. Go through a kissing gate and turn left. Continue to a lane and turn right, COAST PATH BOSSINGTON. Retrace your steps to the car park.

The Ship Inn, Porlock Weir
'The Bottom Ship', as it is known, to distinguish it from 'the Top Ship' in Porlock, built of beach stone with lime mortar, has exposed beams (some are ship's timbers), period photos and lateral chimneystacks.

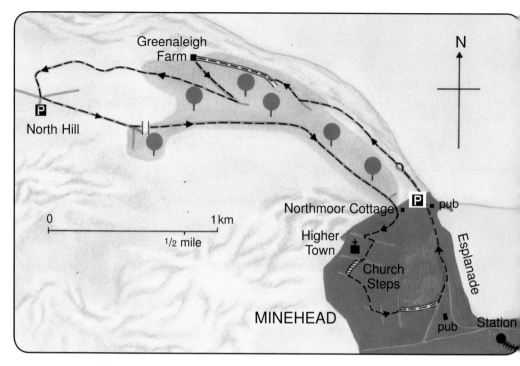

Walk 9 Minehead and North Hill

Distance: 7.8km (4³/₄ miles) Time: 2¹/₂ hours
Character: A long climb through woodland from Minehead's
attractive harbour to North Hill (220m), with a couple of steep
sections, is rewarded with superb views across to Wales, and south
over Exmoor. The latter part of the walk is gently downhill through
woodland to Minehead's historic Higher Town, which has a splendid
church and numerous thatched cottages.

Park towards the western end of the Esplanade or in the Quay Road
West car park. The walk starts at the Ship Aground, beside the harbour. Head away from the town. The road soon ends and there is a
tarmac path parallel to the beach. Later it becomes an earthen path
which heads inexorably uphill. Keep right, COAST PATH, then join a
tarmac track. Continue ahead. There are good views of Greenaleigh
Point below on your right.

Just before you reach Greenaleigh Farm, turn left up steps (COAST
PATH PORLOCK). This climbs steadily at a diagonal to the hillside,
up to a bench. Turn sharp right (COAST PATH) and continue uphill,
emerging onto furze- and bracken-clad cliffs.

When the path doglegs, follow it sharp left, climbing steeply to a footpath junction. Take a rest on the bench to enjoy the views and then turn left towards HIGHERTOWN.

After 600m the path divides into three. Keep left and walk ahead, ignoring side turnings. Descend gently through woodland along the broad path, keeping a low wall and then a wire fence on your right. The path divides at a signpost, indicating NORTH HILL which is where you have walked from. Continue ahead onto the tarmac, past Northmoor Cottage and downhill to a T-junction. Turn left and continue downhill.

Take the next right turn, CHURCH ROAD, and walk down to St Michael's, which displays an illuminated missal dating from 1320, as well as having a carved screen, a clock jack, and much else of interest and beauty.

Turn right at the church gate. Turn left after 25m, down CHURCH STEPS. Walk down past the thatched cottages. Turn left into CHURCH STREET, then left into MIDDLE STREET. Keep right, then turn left into CLANVILLE STREET. At the bottom of this street follow the footpath ahead down to the Esplanade. Turn left (or right for the Hobby Horse) and into Quay Town with its old buildings.

The Hobby Horse Inn (01643) 702274

Originally part of the Metropole Hotel, and partaking in its Victorian opulence, it gets its name from Minehead's May Day Hobby horse celebrations. Ask to see the dining room with its impressive plaster ceiling, and the remarkable Victorian baroque ballroom.

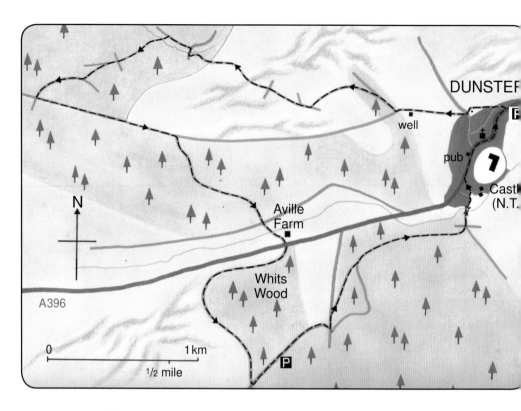

Walk 10   Dunster

Distance: 10km (6¹/₄ miles) Time: 3¹/₂ hours
Character: A demanding exploration of the hills and woods near
Dunster. At the end of the walk, you may wish to explore the town.

Park in the car park at the north end of Dunster (SS993439). Walk towards the town, then, 50m beyond the Visitor Centre, turn right into THE BALL. When the lane turns left, continue ahead (PRIVATE DRIVE – FOOTPATH ACCESS). At the top of the tarmac drive continue ahead on a footpath across a field to the medieval butter cross.

Turn left down ST GEORGE'S STREET. Only 30m ahead, turn right into the bridleway, CONDUIT LANE GRABBIST HILL. Just beyond St Leonard's Well, the path divides at a deer gate. Fork right. After 150m, bear left and head uphill and through a gate. Turn right at the next path junction. Keep left when the path divides, and continue ahead, ALCOMBE, and again, YOUTH HOSTEL.

At a tarred lane, turn right, then after 50m left, TIMBERSCOMBE. The path turns left after 200m, indicated by a blue arrow waymark, crosses

the stream and climbs steeply. Keep left at a fork. Join a track near the top of the slope and continue to a vehicle barrier at a path junction. Turn left here and continue to the path crossing.

Turn left signed DUNSTER. This path offers superb views of the coast and eventually returns to the deer gate near St Leonard's Well. You may wish to shorten the walk in this way. If not, continue on the path for 1 km, then turn right BRIDLEWAY CROYDON HILL.

When the bridleway divides, turn right and steeply downhill at the next blue waymark. Cross the tarred lane. Continue ahead, over the footbridge to the road. Cross with care. Walk ahead, TIMBERSCOMBE.

Follow the path uphill to a gate, then around the edge of Whits Wood. When the path divides, keep ahead, TIMBERSCOMBE. Keep right, TIMBERSCOMBE, at the next division. Turn right again at the next division and walk on to a three-way marker post. This time, don't take the Timberscombe option but turn left, BRIDLEWAY, and continue to a tarred lane.

Turn left and follow the lane downhill past Nutcombe Bottom car park. Do not take the lane to Broadwood Farm. Walk on for 50 m. Bear right DUNSTER. Follow the path uphill, then down through the forest.

Keep ahead, DUNSTER, at the next junction and cross medieval Gallox Bridge. Reaching the entrance to a car park, continue ahead up the footpath to a T-junction. Turn left (unless you wish to visit the mill or its tearooms) and follow the mill leat up to West Street.

Turn right, and you will see the Stag's Head on your left. Continue to the 1499 Priory church and round to the main street, past the Yarn Market (1609) and the medieval Luttrell Arms, to the car park.

The Stag's Head 01643 821229 www.visitdunster.co.uk

A listed medieval building with many interesting features, the Stag's Head began as an open hall-house, the smoke from the open fires simply percolating upwards and out through the roof. In the guest rooms, jointed cruck beams and timber framing are exposed. One room has a fresco and is thought to have a hidden cavity or 'priest-hole' behind. Downstairs are more exposed beams and masonry. Log fires occupy two stone hearths.

Among the period photographs is one of the stag's head being presented to the inn in the early 1960s by the Devon and Somerset Staghounds. The name of the inn was changed at that time from the New Inn. The Stag's Head is a friendly, family-run inn open all year, offering food at lunchtimes (except Thursday) and evenings. In summer there is the beer garden and terrace to enjoy.